1

can　　man　　ran　　van

Little Andy saw a – – –,
He kicked it and it hit a – – –,
Out got a very angry – – –,
So Andy ran, and ran, and – – –.

2

all　　ball　　far　　star

My sister says she will go – – –,
She'll reach the top—she'll be a – – – –,
I don't think she'll go far at – – –,
She can hardly kick a – – – –.

3

confusing　　do　　find　　losing　　mind　　you

Tell me, do you ever – – – –,
Your teacher can't make up her – – – –?
"Sit down," she says, and when you – –,
"Sit up now," she is telling – – –.
Up or down? It's so – – – – – – – – –,
Either way, you end up – – – – – –.

4

Find as many words as you can that rhyme with "**call**".

1   **hip   in   nip   pin**

Suddenly I felt a – – –,
In the area of my – – –,
I felt around and found a – – –,
But I don't know who stuck it – –.

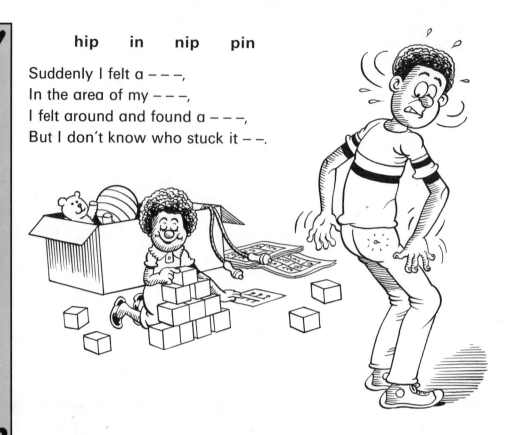

2   **head   him   said   Tim**

Once there was a boy called – – –,
But no one ever spoke to – – –,
Because he had too big a – – – –,
"I'm wonderful," was all he – – – –.

3   **fit   grit   hit   quit**

Jim, the jogger, was fighting – – –,
And sure enough, he had true – – – –,
But by a lorry, he was – – –,
So now his jogging he has – – – –.

4   Make a list of all the words you can think of that rhyme with "**sit**", and then use them to try to make up a verse of your own.

2

1

brim   dim   him   Jim

A gentleman, whose name was – – –,
Though rich, was really rather – – –,
He filled his cup up to the – – – –,
And wondered why tea spilt on – – –.

2

bog   dog   jog   log

An athlete went out for a – – –,
And took with him his faithful – – –,
They both tripped over a fallen – – –,
And landed face-down in a – – –.

3

for   not   shot   war

The soldier was in hiding – – –,
He didn't want to go to – – –.
Some men like fighting—he does – – –,
He does not fancy being – – – –.

4

How many words can you find to rhyme with "**frog**"?

3

1

chump   lump   plump   thump

I really did not deserve that – – – – –,
I didn't say that you were – – – – –,
I only asked about that – – – –,
That you have in your jumper, you – – – – –.

2

bug   chum   done   drug   Mum   one

Poor old Jimmy caught a – – –,
The doctor prescribed a wonder – – – –
To cure him, but when it was – – – –,
Jimmy caught another – – –.
He's fed up staying in with – – –,
So he gave the second bug to his – – – –.

3

blood   cut   mud   rut

His bicycle wheel caught in a – – –,
He fell and thought his knee was – – –,
He looked to see if there was – – – – –,
He couldn't see it for the – – –.

4

See how many words you can find that rhyme with "**fun**".

1

expired   mile   tired   while

Dad said he could run a – – – –,
He hadn't done it for a – – – – –,
At fifty metres, he was – – – – –,
After a hundred, he nearly – – – – – – –.

2

fate   plate   name   came   gaze
daze   shake   take   dare   everywhere
wane   brain   delay   away

The witch put Mary on a – – – – –,
To be eaten was her – – – –,
When suddenly a fairy – – – –,
And gently whispered Mary's – – – –.
Mary looked up in a – – – –,
And met the fairy's gentle – – – –.
The fairy told her, she must – – – –
The pot of pepper—she must – – – – –
The spicy pepper – – – – – – – – – –,
For she knew witches do not – – – –
To sneeze—it damages their – – – – –,
And makes their magic power – – – –,
So Mary acted right – – – –,
Then ran off home without – – – – –.

3

Write down what you think Mary told her mother when she asked
Mary where she had been.

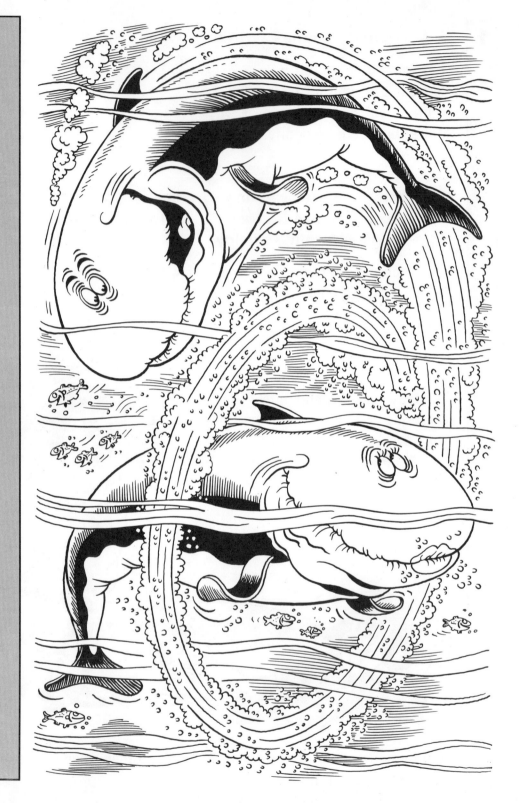

1

whale	tale	female	stale	dame	blame
sage	rage	grade	parade	fade	Jade
lake	take	gape	shape	stare	rare
cave	wave	gaze	daze	male	gale

I'd like to tell you now the – – – –,
Of Willowby, the lovesick – – – – –,
Who felt his life was getting – – – – –,
For want of his own young – – – – – –.
There wasn't anyone to – – – – –,
That he could never find a – – – –,
He didn't fly into a – – – –,
Instead, he sought the ocean – – – –,
Who organised a whale – – – – – –,
To see if Willowby made the – – – – –,
With a lovely lady whale called – – – –,
Whose beauty wouldn't ever – – – –.
The route the whale parade would – – – –,
Would pass up through a deep sea – – – –,
The sage was sure Jade's lovely – – – – –,
Would make young Willowby's whale mouth – – – –,
And sure enough, her beauty – – – –,
Made Willowby both stop and – – – – –:
He flipped for joy and made a – – – –,
And took Jade with him to his – – – –,
And swam about in happy – – – –,
His dear Jade never left his – – – –.
In calmest days or in a – – – –,
Of whales, he was the happiest – – – –.

2 Make up a title for this poem, and then write about what you think happened to Jade and Willowby later.

1

five   hive   shame   tame

Once a little boy of – – – –,
Put his hand inside a – – – –,
A big bee stung him—what a – – – – –,
And he had thought that bees were – – – –.

2

awoke   bore   more   poke

One Sunday morning, I – – – – –
My dear old father with a – – – –,
He turned round, snored, and slept some – – – –,
Fathers sometimes are a – – – –.

3

dope   Jove   soap   stove

The colonel looked and said, "By – – – –!
What's that you're cooking on the – – – – –?"
But I was boiling towels in – – – –,
If he eats that, he'll feel a – – – –.

4

Find the rhyming pairs of words:
    sore   bite   bone   bright   door   stone

1

avoid boy corduroy destroyed
joy toy

My gran has a picture of Dad as a – – –,
All dressed up in a suit of – – – – – – – –,
His hair is all curly, he's holding a – – –,
When she shows it, it soon puts an end to his – – –.
Dad thinks that the picture should be – – – – – – – –,
But that, at all costs, my gran will – – – – –.

2

bow cow how vow

A little monster made a – – –,
To turn his friend into a – – –,
He seemed to know exactly – – –,
When his friend mooed, he took a – – –.

3

fowl howl owl yowl

Once there was a silly – – – –,
Who thought he was a wise old – – –,
And all day long he'd sit and – – – –,
He couldn't hoot, but he could – – – –.

4

Make a list of all the words you can find that rhyme with "**crown**".

9

1

awe   saw   shawl   wall

When I peeped through the keyhole, what I – – –,
Filled my heart and mind with – – –,
A poor old lady in a – – – – –,
Was handcuffed to the cellar – – – –.

2

brawl   draw   drawl   raw

Bill, the boaster, would brag and – – – – –,
How he'd won the latest – – – – –,
When I saw him, his fists were – – –,
I would say it was a – – – –.

3

boat   float   goat   overcoat

A silly little billy – – – –,
Thought one day that he could – – – – –,
Down-river on an – – – – – – – –,
He really should have used a – – – –.

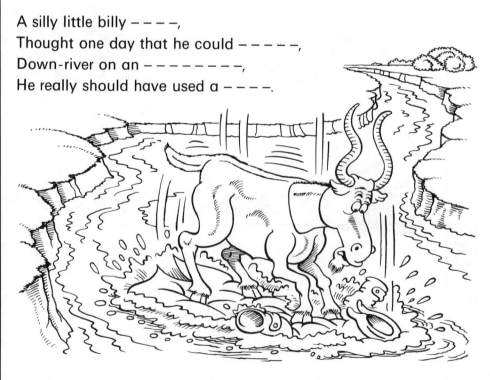

4

Find as many words as you can that rhyme with "**fear**" and then
use them to make up your own verse.

1

feel   real   teeth   underneath

I wonder if his hair is – – – –,
I'd dearly love to have a – – – –,
I think he is bald – – – – – – – – – –,
I wonder if he has false – – – – –?

2

bean   heap   leap   lean

A Mexican once tried to – – – –,
On a giant jumping – – – –,
The jumping bean began to – – – –,
The Mexican fell in a – – – –.

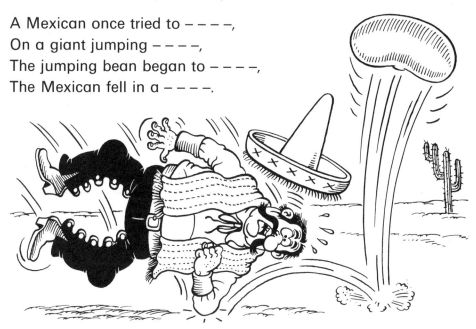

3

**hair   fair   again   rain   complained
stained**

She didn't like it being – – – –,
And so she tried to dye her – – – –,
But when she went out in the – – – –,
Her hair came back to fair – – – – –,
But now her face was dark and – – – – – – –,
She took the dye back and – – – – – – – – – –.

4

Write down at least six words that contain "**ee**".

1

hair   chair   chain   rain   wail   fail
quaint   paint   saint   faint   complain
disdain   tail   jail   brain   vain

He tied his granny to her – – – – –,
He tied a knot in baby's – – – –,
He splashed through puddles in the – – – –,
He tied his friend up with a – – – – –,
And every day, he'd never – – – –,
To tease the cat and make it – – – –.
He daubed the dog with blobs of – – – – –,
He thought it made the dog look – – – – – –.
He made the teachers feel quite – – – – –,
He'd try the patience of a – – – – –.
He looked on neighbours with – – – – – – –,
If ever they tried to – – – – – – – –.
But then his dad came out of – – – –,
At once he kicked his bad son's – – – –.
The punishment was not in – – – –,
At last he's learned to use his – – – – –.

2

How many words can you find that rhyme with "**chained**"?

12

1

hay   Neigh   say   today

The comic said, "I say, I – – –!
A funny thing happened – – – – –.
My mother-in-law was eating – – –,
I asked for some, but she said, '– – – – –!'"

2

bray   clay   May   way

A sculptress once whose name was – – –
Made a donkey out of – – – –,
She worked in such a clever – – –,
You could almost hear the donkey – – – –.

3

balloon   book   look   soon

He flew away in his hot air – – – – – – –,
I think he will be coming back – – – –,
You see, he forgot to take the – – – –,
That tells how to fly it—here he comes— – – – –.

4

Find as many words as you can that rhyme with "**playing**".

13

1

around   cloud   proud   sound

I thought I heard some music – – – – –,
I stopped to listen and looked – – – – – –,
And there above me, looking – – – – –,
An angel played his harp on a – – – – –.

2

doubt   house   mouse   shout

I'd really like to be a – – – – –,
And live in a deserted – – – – –,
It would be peaceful, there's no – – – – –,
With no grown-ups to scold and – – – – –.

3

blue   hue   true   view

He said his new pet dog was – – – –,
Would you believe that that was – – – –?
Skye Terriers may be of that – – –,
But not Red Setters in my – – –.–.

4

How many words can you find that rhyme with "**glue**"?

1

chewed   new   renewed   stew

For years and years he chewed and – – – – – – –,
His teeth were worn, they needed – – – – – – –,
But when he got his false teeth – – –,
He chewed more easily on his – – – –.

2

crew   few   grew   slew

Of great adventures I've had a – – –,
But when I fought the pirate – – – –,
And every single one I – – – –,
My reputation grew and – – – –.

3

brew   dew   grew   Kew

At the gardens known as – – –,
A tiny little drop of – – –
Fell on a flower, and how it – – – –!
Could it have been a magic – – – –?

4

See how many words you can find that rhyme with "**brewing**".

1

flew   threw   Timbuktu   view

An Australian in the outback – – – – –,
A boomerang and off it – – – –,
It disappeared right out of – – – –,
And came back via – – – – – – – –.

2

kipper   sea   skipper   ship

"I'd like to sail on a sailing – – – –,
I'd like to be the – – – – – – –."
"What do you know about the – – –?
You've got as much brain as a – – – – – –."

3

flat   ship   slip   that

Columbus knew the world was not – – – –,
Though most thought it was—now fancy – – – –!
They thought that if they sailed on a – – – –,
Eventually over the edge they would – – – –.

4

Write a list of all the words you can think of that start with "**sk**".

1

crept   inept   kept   wept

Raymond, the goalie, felt – – – – –,
The ball into the goal had – – – – –
Between his feet—if only he'd – – – –
His feet together, he needn't have – – – –.

2

gold   bold   sword   lord
aunt   can't   barred   hard

I'd like to be a pirate – – – –,
And rob the galleons of their – – – –,
I'd wear an eye-patch and a – – – – –,
And buy a castle like a – – – –.
I'd like to do that, but I – – –'–,
Unless I get leave from my – – – –,
And really, she is pretty – – – –,
She'll rule that piracy is – – – – – –.

3

Make a list of words that rhyme with "**drink**" and then use them to make up your own verse.

1

around   dump   hump   pound

Rafi was going to the – – – –,
Loads of rubbish he had to – – – –,
When on the road he saw a – – – – –,
He dropped his rubbish all – – – – – –.

2

fast   felt   knelt   vast

When on the drawing pin I – – – – –,
A tiny little stab I – – – –,
Then all at once, the pain was – – – –,
That made me get up very – – – –.

3

course   horse   much   such

Lord Mickey was not rich as – – – –,
But he gambled far too – – – –.
He bet his shirt upon a – – – – –,
And had to go home bare of – – – – – –.

4

How many words can you find that rhyme with "**change**"?

1

beard   learn   stern   weird

The teachers here are very – – – – –,
They keep on forcing me to – – – – –,
The one we have is very – – – – –,
She has a moustache and a – – – – –.

2

back   black   rack   smack

When Billy brought her false teeth – – – –,
His granny gave him quite a – – – – –.
If he had left them on the – – – –,
The white bits wouldn't all be – – – – –.

3

deck   neck   speck   wreck

The sailors polished up the – – – –,
The captain said, "You've left a – – – – –."
He soon became a total – – – – –,
Because he slipped and broke his – – – –.

4

Find as many words as you can that rhyme with "**spank**".

19

1

nipping   skipping   tripping   whipping

The little puppy dog was – – – – – –,
The heels of a girl, while she was – – – – – – – –.
He did not stop till she was – – – – – – – –,
His master gave him quite a – – – – – – – –.

2

chipped   dripped   ripped   sipped

The shabby old tramp some cold tea – – – – – –,
From a dirty old cup, that was cracked and – – – – – – –,
Down his chin, the cold tea – – – – – – –,
And on to his coat, which was tattered and – – – – – –.

3

bluffed   spotted   stuffed   trotted

We were sure he only – – – – – – –,
When he said the lion was – – – – – – –,
Just as well his trick we – – – – – – –,
The lion roared and off we – – – – – – –.

4

See how many words you can find that rhyme with **"dripping"**.

20

1

clapped   hissed   missed   tapped

The football fans all jeered and – – – – – –,
When the penalty kick he – – – – – –,
But when the rebound he skilfully – – – – – –,
Into the goal, they cheered and – – – – – – –.

2

kidding   skidding   sobbing   throbbing

Amanda thought her friend was – – – – – – –,
When she said the bus was – – – – – – – –,
But suddenly her heart was – – – – – – – – –,
The bus skidded past and left her – – – – – – –.

3

banned   flogged   manned   slogged

The poor slaves in the galley – – – – – – –,
And if they chatted, they were – – – – – – –,
Every ship like this was – – – – – –,
I'm glad that slavery has been – – – – – –.

4

Make a list of all the words you can find that rhyme with **"carry"**.

21

1

bright   fight   guy   high   knight   plight

I think I'd like to be a – – – – – –,
In silver armour, shining – – – – – –,
With sword and shield I'd have to – – – – –,
To save a fair maid from her – – – – – –,
I'd rescue her from tower – – – –,
She'd say I was a real brave – – –.

2

buying   denying   lying   spying

Pete, the policeman, went out – – – – – –
On Bill, the burglar, who was – – – – –,
When in court, he was – – – – – – –,
Stealing things, instead of – – – – – –.

3

awry   by   dye   try

Silly Billy thought he'd – – –,
To change his cat to green with – – –,
Unluckily it went – – – –,
Bill's green, and his friends pass him – –.

4

Find as many words as you can to rhyme with "**tight**".

**cried   died   cry   die   denied   replied
tried   magnified   decried   satisfied
lied   vilified   mortified   implied
pacified   dried   wise   eyes**

When her pet, the hamster, – – – –,
Marie cried and cried and – – – – –.
Her mother said that, when pets – – –,
It's natural that you should – – –.
But Marie, sobbing, then – – – – – – –,
"There's one thing that can't be – – – – – –,
My grief, my pain is – – – – – – – – –,
Because I never really – – – – –,
To keep my hamster – – – – – – – – –,
My laziness should be – – – – – – –,
Indeed, I should be – – – – – – – – –,
To tell the truth, I sometimes – – – –,
That I had fed him, I – – – – – – –,
And now I feel quite – – – – – – – – –."
But mother soothed her, and she – – – – –
Her tears away, and – – – – – – – –
Her daughter, saying, "Dry your – – – –,
And let this lesson make you – – – –."

Write down all the words you can find that rhyme with "**trying**".

23

1

blaring   consuming   fuming   glaring

Our Headteacher, she is – – – – – –,
With a rage that's all- – – – – – – – – –,
She's turned red, her eyes are – – – – – – –,
I only set the fire bell – – – – – –.

2

**amazing   blazing   boring   ignoring
filing   piling**

The typist was no good at – – – – – –,
All around, papers were – – – – – –,
She found filing pretty – – – – – –,
So the papers she's – – – – – – – – –,
Her annual tidy-up's – – – – – – –,
She just sets the whole lot – – – – – –.

3

**aching   commentating   congratulating
taking**

People were – – – – – – – – – – – – – – –,
Archie on his – – – – – – – – – – – –,
He did not hear them, he was – – – – – –
His microphone off—his tongue was – – – – – –.

4

How many words can you find that rhyme with "**smoking**"?

amazing   gazing   invading   fading
caring   staring   taking   quaking
flaring   daring   escaping   gaping
making   shaking   raving   waving

As I was through my window – – – – – –,
I saw a vision so – – – – – – –,
Sometimes bright and sometimes – – – – – –,
A space ship—could they be – – – – – – – –,
These little green men who were – – – – – – –?
No—they really looked quite – – – – – –.
I really felt I should be – – – – – – –,
But I was calm, and I was – – – – – –
Steps towards them—that was – – – – – –!
Suddenly the ship was – – – – – – –,
I stood still—my mouth was – – – – – –,
I should really be – – – – – – – –.
All at once the ship was – – – – – – –,
The little green men started – – – – – –
Movements that looked quite like – – – – – –,
If I tell Dad, he'll say I'm – – – – – –.

Find as many words as you can that rhyme with "**icing**".

1

consternation   extermination   illustration
imagination

The teacher said, "Use your – – – – – – – – – – –,
When I ask you for an – – – – – – – – – – – –."
I did and it caused me much – – – – – – – – – – – – –,
I drew him—he's threatening my – – – – – – – – – – – –.

2

condition   decision   division   submission

The wrestler from the heavy – – – – – – – –,
Challenged the skinny man, out of – – – – – – – – –,
The skinny man easily got the – – – – – – – –,
He tickled the heavyweight into – – – – – – – – – –.

3

apprehension   detention   explanation
multiplication

Can you imagine my – – – – – – – – – – – –,
When teacher told me to stay for – – – – – – – – –?
My father will need a good – – – – – – – – – – –,
Like, "I volunteered for more – – – – – – – – – – – – –."

4

Can you find at least six words that end with "**ation**"?

potion   notion   motion   lotion
satisfaction   distraction   reaction   action
nation   animation   isolation   preparation
comprehension   tension   termination
consideration   decision   condition   fiction
restriction   imagination   indication

Silly Billy had a n – – – – –,
He could make a magic p – – – – –,
He could use it as a l – – – – –
So he set his plans in m – – – – –
Worked on them without d – – – – – – – – –
And it gave much s – – – – – – – – – – –,
For when it went into a – – – – –,
It produced a strange r – – – – – – –,
Of suspended a – – – – – – – –,
He suspended all the n – – – – –,
Using up his p – – – – – – – – – –,
Left himself in i – – – – – – – –,
Loneliness then caused him t – – – – – –,
Far beyond his c – – – – – – – – – – – –,
After some c – – – – – – – – – – – –,
He decided t – – – – – – – – – –,
Of the nation's still c – – – – – – – –
Seemed to be the best d – – – – – – –,
So he lifted the r – – – – – – – – – –.
If you think that this is f – – – – – –,
I think that's an i – – – – – – – – –,
You have no i – – – – – – – – – –.

Try to find at least six words that end with "**action**".

27

1

anywhere   **box**   **place**   **there**

She put her jewels in a – – –,
They would be safe in – – – – –,
She put the box in a very safe – – – – –,
Now she can't find her jewels – – – – – – – –.

2

fun   **sun**   **glad**   **bad**   **day**   **play**   **away**

On Monday I went out because
    there was some lovely – – –,
On Tuesday I went out because
    I needed lots of – – –,
On Wednesday I went out because
    the rain was not too – – –,
On Thursday I went out because
    the rain stopped—I was – – – –,
On Friday I went out because
    I wanted out to – – – –,
On Saturday I went out because
    the rain might go – – – –,

On Sunday I got the measles and had to stay in on
Monday, Tuesday, Wednesday, Thursday, Friday, Saturday
and Sunday and the sun shone every – – –.

3

Write down what you like doing best on every day of the week.

28

1

fidget   hedging   midget   sledging

One day a little − − − − − −,
Decided to go − − − − − − − −.
You should have seen him − − − − − −
When his sledge wedged in the − − − − − − −.

2

bikes   for   likes   war

Excitement is what Bobby − − − − −,
Exciting things like motor − − − − −,
Exciting games like battles, − − −,
Excitement is what he lives − − −.

3

car   stage   star   wage

I'd like to be successful at acting on the − − − − −,
I'd like to be successful and earn a great big − − − −,
And if I'm not successful at being a big − − − −,
I hope I'll be successful enough to buy a fancy − − −.

4

Write down the things that you find most exciting.

29

1

king   knock-out   ring   wrestler

I'd like to be a – – – – – – – –,
And wrestle in a – – – –,
Then I would do a – – – – – –·– –,
And walk round like a – – – –.

2

kneel   squeal   thistle   was

I knelt upon a – – – – – – –,
It made me writhe and – – – – – –,
I gnashed my teeth, and thought that – – –
The dumbest place to – – – – –.

3

beautiful   own   squiggle   wriggle

Her writing is always – – – – – – – – –,
She never does a – – – – – – – –,
My pencil has a mind of its – – –,
And always wants to – – – – – – –.

4

Find as many words as you can that begin with "**gn**".

1

arms   sailor   sea   tea

Did you ever see a – – – – – –,
Sailing on the – – –,
With muscles on his great big – – – –,
And mussels for his – – –?

2

amount   day   tot   weigh

The teacher taught the tiny – – –,
To read and write and – – – – –,
She taught the tot the right – – – – – –,
To make his way one – – –.

3

ate   creature   flour   hour

We bred our little – – – – – – – –,
And fed it bread and – – – – –,
It didn't like that, so it – – –,
Eight sunflowers every – – – –.

4

Write down these words and then write a word beside each of them which sounds the same, but is spelt differently:

sew   bored   week   tail   hare
sight   one

1 The rhymes on this page are all mixed up. Can you sort them out?

A little kitten once was lost,
It sparkled and it glowed,
Wearing jodhpurs and a cap,
As it drove along the road.

Mary loved to ride a horse,
With sausages and ham,
It dazzled passing drivers,
And had some bread and jam.

Mother cooked a lovely tea,
At the break of day,
Its fur was black, its eyes were green,
On each school holiday.

I went to wash the car one day,
It was all soft and sweet,
I ate it up and licked my lips,
And it had four white feet.

2 See if you can make up four rhymes and do the same with them.

TLS 4

EVA'S STORY

A survivor's tale by the step-sister
of Anne Frank

Eva Schloss
with
Evelyn Julia Kent

CASTLE-KENT

Published in 1992
by
Castle-Kent
49 Dorset Drive, Edgware, Middlesex HA8 7NT

First published in Great Britain by
W. H. Allen & Co. Plc 1988

Printed and bound in Great Britain by
Cox & Wyman Ltd, Reading, Berks.

ISBN 0 9518865 0 9

Author's note: This is a true story. As it is told from memory, some of the incidental detail may not always be quite accurate.

British Library Cataloguing-in-Publication Data.
A catalogue record for this book is available from the British Library.

To my daughters Caroline, Jacky and Sylvia, and to my father Erich and my brother Heinz, whom they never knew, with the hope that this book will bring them closer.

In every ghetto, in every deportation train, in every
labour camp, even in the death camps, the will to
resist was strong and took many forms; fighting
with those few weapons that could be found,
fighting with sticks and knives, individual acts of
defiance and protest, the courage of obtaining food
under the threat of death, the nobility of refusing to
allow the Germans their final wish to gloat over
panic and despair. Even passivity was a form of
resistance. 'Not to act,' Emanuel Ringelblum wrote
in the aftermath of one particularly savage reprisal,
'not to lift a hand against the Germans, has become
the quiet passive heroism of the common Jew.' To
die with dignity was a form of resistance. To resist
the dehumanizing, brutalizing force of evil, to
refuse to be abased to the level of animals, to live
through the torment, to outlive the tormentors,
these too were resistance. Merely to give witness by
one's own testimony was, in the end, to contribute
to a moral victory. Simply to survive was a victory
of the human spirit.

– Martin Gilbert,
The Holocaust: A Jewish Tragedy (Collins, 1986)